DEATH EATERS

Meet Nature's Scavengers

KELLY MILNER HALLS

Ⓜ Millbrook Press • Minneapolis

To my daughter Kerry, who, like her mom, always wondered about the facts of life and death. To my daughter Vanessa, who is about to study entomology (bugs). And to Liz, my favorite weirdo.

Acknowledgments: Much appreciation to Dr. Jon R. Thogmartin, Chief Medical Examiner, Largo, Florida; Dr. Gail S. Anderson, School of Criminology, Simon Fraser University, Burnaby, British Columbia, Canada; Alana Inks, Spokane County Medical Examiner's Office, Spokane, Washington; and Dr. Jennifer L. Pechal, Department of Entomology, Michigan State University, East Lansing, Michigan, for their time, expertise, and generosity. I am so grateful.

Millbrook Press
A division of Lerner Publishing Group, Inc.
241 First Avenue North
Minneapolis, MN 55401 USA

For reading levels and more information, look up this title at www.lernerbooks.com.

Main body text set in Caecilia LT Std 11/16. Typeface provided by Adobe Systems.

Library of Congress Cataloging-in-Publication Data

Names: Halls, Kelly Milner, 1957– author.
Title: Death eaters : meet nature's scavengers / by Kelly Milner Halls.
Description: Minneapolis : Millbrook Press, [2018] | Audience: Ages 9–14. | Audience: Grades 4 to 6. | Includes
    bibliographical references and index. Identifiers: LCCN 2017040493 (print) | LCCN 2017043634 (ebook) |
    ISBN 9781541524736 (eb pdf) | ISBN 9781512482003 (lb : alk. paper)
Subjects: LCSH: Death (Biology)—Juvenile literature. | Biodegradation—Juvenile literature. | Scavengers
    (Zoology)—Juvenile literature.
Classification: LCC QH530.5 (ebook) | LCC QH530.5 .H35 2018 (print) | DDC 591.7/14—dc23

LC record available at https://lccn.loc.gov/2017040493

Manufactured in the United States of America
1-43222-33013-3/30/2018

Contents

DEATH—AN IMPORTANT PART OF LIFE

Life on Earth has thrived for almost four billion years. But an individual life of a human or an animal doesn't last *that* long. As one generation of creatures passes away, another is born to take its place—that's the cycle of life.

But what happens to all the bodies of those dead humans and animals? Why aren't we surrounded by four billion years' worth of dead stuff? Why aren't we climbing mountains of corpses or trudging through fields of lifeless insects?

The answer is simple: recycling. When life ends, the body is consumed by an incredibly efficient ecosystem—a powerful team of death eaters. Scavengers and decomposers work together to break apart the nutrients of the dead carcass to reuse in their own lives or to provide for new life.

What kinds of creatures are members of this cleanup crew? And how do these death eaters contribute to decomposition? It might seem disgusting to explore how dead bodies are devoured, but decomposition is a scientific marvel our world literally *could not* live without. Sure, it's gross, but it is also amazing.

In 2016, 322 reindeer were found dead in Norway. Scientists believe lightning killed them. Luckily, nature has its own cleanup crew—death eaters.

Chapter 1

LIFE AFTER DEATH

How does decomposition begin? It starts with death. Imagine a wild boar wandering through a forest in winter. It has lived a long life, but its joints ache and pop, and its old heart struggles to pump blood. Weary to its core, the boar finds a final resting place. Drifting off into a peaceful sleep, its heart stops.

The old boar has died. Its lifeless body feels nothing. In the hours and days to come, the boar's carcass will go through many changes as it decomposes. And many different kinds of death eaters will step in to help.

THE FIVE STAGES OF DECOMPOSITION

When a vertebrate—an animal that has a spine and a skeleton—dies, its body goes through five general stages of decomposition. How quickly a body passes through each phase depends on factors such as temperature, exposure to wind and rain, and proximity to other animals.

Stage 1: Fresh

The initial moments after the wild boar's death launch the first stage of decomposition referred to as the fresh phase. Without a pulsing heart to pump blood, the dead body is denied oxygen and autolysis begins.

Autolysis is self-digestion—enzymes team up with intestinal bacteria to begin breaking down the body from the inside. An enzyme is a chemical substance in plants and animals that helps assist natural processes such as digestion. The enzymes break apart the cells they once lived in while the microscopic bacteria that live in the intestines (and normally help the boar digest its food) begin digesting the body's soft tissue.

Stage 2: Bloat

Within about three days, the soft tissue within the boar's body is reduced to a swirl of fluids and gases trapped by layers and layers of skin. Because blood is no longer circulating, the skin turns a pale or ashen color.

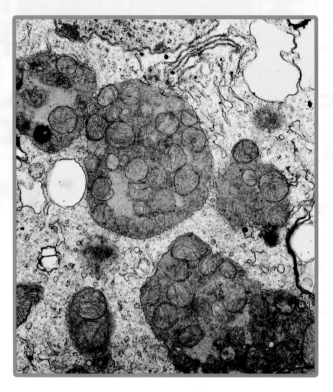

These cells contain hydrolase enzymes, which break apart a body's cells when the body dies.

Red blood cells

WHY DOES DEAD SKIN LOOK DIFFERENT?

Have you ever felt your cheeks blush? Medical experts call it vasodilation. Your brain tells your body you're embarrassed—or hot—so it floods your face with blood to cool you down. When a heart stops beating, blood no longer circulates to keep skin warm and vibrant. Gravity causes it to pool at the body's lowest point. Without blood, the skin changes to a pale or ashen color.

When the boar was alive, gases—produced by digestive bacteria—were expelled naturally from the body. In death, that isn't possible. So like a balloon, the body swells. This phase of decomposition is bloat. If the weather is cool, the swelling is slower. If the weather is hot, more gas is produced and the bloat speeds up. Eventually, the skin tears and the gas begins to escape. And it does *not* smell good.

Stage 3: Active Decay

Some scientists say the smell of decomposition is sickly sweet, like a plastic bag full of warm, rotten fruit. Others compare it to a recipe of spoiled meat, dirty diapers, or a full dumpster on a hot summer day. All agree it's a powerfully *bad* smell most people would rather not experience. But the strong odor is irresistible to insects—they bring in the next stage of decomposition: active decay. In this stage, insects feed on the flesh of the boar's carcass until most of the soft tissue is gone.

THE SCIENCE OF STINK

When experts study the science of decomposition, they often study scents—such as the strong smell of esters (when acid and other elements combine to release liquids). By observing human bodies called cadavers, scientists can focus on the smell of decomposition.

If human bodies aren't available, pigs make good substitutes—pigs and humans have eight esters in common.

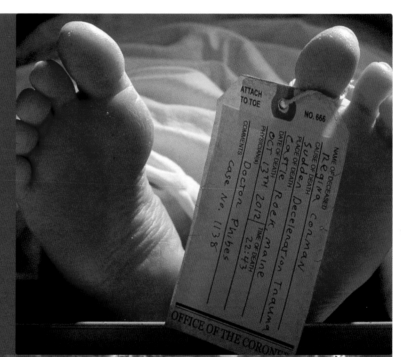

Stage 4: Advanced Decay

When most of the soft, wet flesh has been eaten, insects leave the boar's body. Animals that feed on the dead, called scavengers, arrive to eat the remaining few pieces of flesh. If an animal finds the boar soon after it dies, however, it will not let the insects have all the fun—as long as there is no immediate threat from a larger animal nearby, the scavenger will eat as much of the boar as it can.

Stage 5: Dry Remains

At the final stage of decomposition—dry remains—the flesh is completely gone. All that remains of the old boar's body is a pile of dried bones, teeth, hair, and cartilage. Other animals, rain, or wind might scatter these leftovers, bringing bits of the boar to new places.

WHY DOES THE SMELL OF DEATH MATTER?

Consider the difficult work of rescue dogs. During a disaster such as an earthquake or a tsunami, human and animal lives are endangered. If a rescue dog knows the difference between the smell of the living and the dead and the difference between humans and other animals, it will know which smells to seek out first. Search for the living people first, then living animals, and then the bodies of the lost. If scientists can pinpoint exactly what a dead human smells like, one day they might be able to program machines to replace rescue dogs.

This rescue dog searches for survivors in the aftermath of an earthquake that took place in Mexico City in 2017.

Chapter 2

CREEPY-CRAWLY DEATH EATERS

Decomposition would take a lot more time without the help of death eaters.
These scavengers and decomposers play an important role: they recycle nutrients from the dead
body and bring them back into the ecosystem.

Scavengers such as insects and other animals reach the carcass first. They eat the nutrient-
rich flesh, which allows them to live longer and continue their species through reproduction.
Scavengers of all sizes and species are members of the death-eater cleanup crew. But insects
typically find the dead body first. And flies lead the charge.

BLOWFLIES

Green, iridescent blowflies are important players in decomposition. The eggs they lay will hatch
and break down the body's flesh. But the entire adult life span of a blowfly lasts just seven to
twenty days. They have a lot to do in a short time.

Blowflies must find enough food to stay alive. They must also find suitable mates. And they must lay fertile eggs in nutrient-rich places to guarantee their species will live on. What is the perfect home for a blowfly egg? A moist dead body! Why? Because it provides ample nutrients. Lucky for them, a blowfly's sense of smell is so acute that it can detect a dead body just fifteen minutes after death.

Once the egg-laden female fly finds a carcass, she hovers above the body, looking for wet access. Ears, eyes, and noses are popular options. So are open wounds. Once she picks her spot, she will lay up to three hundred eggs in just seconds. In a single day, blowfly larvae will hatch from the eggs. Most people call these larvae maggots.

The squirming, cream-colored creatures are born to eat. On one end of their bodies are hungry mouths equipped with two sharp hooks to shred decaying flesh into miniature scraps. As blowfly maggots gather the flesh, their large salivary glands release digestive enzymes to liquefy the food.

On the other end of their bodies are tiny spiracles. These spiracles allow the maggots to eat and breathe at the same time, which is vital because they feed twenty-four hours a day. They rarely sleep. When they do, it's for just minutes. Then it's back to gobbling goo.

Top: *Blowflies are one of the most abundant death eaters.*

Middle: *This female blowfly lays her eggs on the flesh of a dead fish. If she cannot find a dead body, she will lay her eggs on animal feces.*

Bottom: *A blowfly goes through its entire life cycle in just seven to twenty days.*

LIFE CYCLE OF A BLOWFLY

ADULT
EGGS
FEEDING LARVAE
WANDERING LARVAE
PUPAE

Multiple blowfly mothers lay their eggs in a carcass. Then the maggots travel as a large group through the decaying body. Hundreds of thousands strong, they wriggle and feed. In less than a week, they can consume more than half of a human body.

A SMELLY IMPOSTER

The corpse flower is no ordinary flower—she blooms very infrequently. It can take years for her blossoms to unfold. But once they do, they smell like death. To flies and beetles, it smells like the perfect place to raise a family.

The corpse flower's smell and color—a deep reddish purple—is supposed to fool insects into thinking it's a dead body. The insects arrive to lay their eggs and then leave when they realize it's not a body. But the pollen of the corpse flower gets on the flies, so they spread the flower's pollen when they leave, continuing the species of the corpse flower.

Like this corpse flower from the US Botanic Garden Conservatory in Washington, DC, in 2013, corpse flowers can stand 10 to 15 feet (3 to 4.6 m) tall when in full bloom.

When the maggots have eaten enough, they leave the dead body to settle into the soil to become pupae—which is much like a butterfly's chrysalis. Days later, they emerge as adult blowflies to start the cycle again. But they are not the only insect death eaters on the prowl. Others soon join the feast.

PILL BUGS

The scent of a decaying corpse is like a beacon to one of the most well-known crustaceans on the planet and one not normally thought of as a death eater—the kid-friendly pill bug.

Most people have playfully handled the armored, fourteen-legged roly-poly without a concern—and without a clue. Sure, they eat rotting plant life. They even clean dangerous metals from gardens and flower beds. But when the opportunity comes, pill bugs also eat the liquefied flesh that spills from a carcass.

Top: Thousands of blowfly maggots can feast on a single dead animal.

Bottom: Despite being just 0.75 inches (1.9 cm) long, pill bugs are versatile death eaters.

But pill bugs do more than just feed on the liquid that comes from inside corpses. In May 2012, after placing a human cadaver under a protective cage at the Forensic Anthropology Center in San Marcos, Texas, scientists discovered that pill bugs nibble on human flesh too. They crawl across the faded skin of the corpse and eat, leaving tiny, near-invisible marks.

"Had we not seen it in the act," scientist Jennifer L. Pechal explained, "it probably would have gone unnoticed. Pill bugs are opportunists, but in all my years of working in forensics, this was the only time I had ever seen one feeding on a human body." What looked like the prick of a needle was actually the nip of a pill bug. Scientists don't know exactly how often pill bugs eat the dead, but they're working to find out more. These death eaters are cute but full of surprises!

BURYING BEETLES

Orange-and-black burying beetles use a different approach as death eaters. They work underground. When the male catches a whiff of a recently deceased animal, he finds a mate. Together the beetles burrow beneath the animal's body, and they start to dig. In just a few hours, they hide a carcass three hundred times their combined weight from view—up to 1 foot (0.3 m) underground. Other scavengers may smell the scent of death, but they can no longer see it.

A burying beetle and its larvae. About thirty species live in the United States and Canada.

A COFFIN FLY'S PRIVATE FEAST

Coffin flies—often mistaken for fruit flies—are death eaters too. But they gather their food after a human body is buried.

"They are particularly talented at getting into sealed places holding decaying matter," says Mohamed Noor, biology professor at Duke University, "including coffins." Coffin flies detect the scent of death in graves and then burrow down to eat the tissues of a corpse and lay eggs in peace. Because coffin flies can get into sealed coffins to feed on dead humans, they have complete privacy since other insects haven't found the bodies.

Several generations of coffin flies can thrive on a single corpse. Scientists estimate the age of a corpse based on how much damage has been done by the flies. Eventually, newly hatched adult coffin flies dig their way back to the surface to find a new corpse.

Safe underground, the couple scrapes all the fur from the animal's skin and then slathers it in spit. Burying beetle spit preserves the flesh just long enough for the female to lay about a dozen eggs inside the body—up to thirty if the dead animal is large.

For about a week, the carcass is both home and nourishment for the growing beetle family. The female eats scraps of flesh and then spits it into the larvae mouths as predigested baby food. While she tends to the larvae, the male guards their hidden home from above. Stuffed to the max, the larvae soon burrow into holes of their own to become pupae. They emerge as fully grown burying beetles forty-five to sixty days later, and then they set off to live as adult beetles.

MEAT ANTS—BUGS EATING BUGS

Australia is home to another kind of death eater—the meat ant. While the red-and-black insects will harvest the meat of a dead rat or lizard, their primary job in the ecosystem of Australia is to clean up dead bugs.

Supercolonies of the dominant ant species set out at dawn in search of insects that died the night before. The meat ants systematically butcher the bodies and carry them home in small pieces. Then they use the body parts to feed every member of their desert colony as well as the root systems of nearby plants.

Meat ants have a forceful, defensive bite. But they have little interest in human beings.

Meat ants move a grasshopper leg into their nest.

Chapter 3

FURRY DEATH EATERS

Insects aren't the only death eaters, however. With decomposition in full swing, the smell of death fills the air. And hungry mammals follow the scent.

Mammals of all shapes and sizes are members of nature's cleanup crew. They live in all different environments, such as the plains of Australia, the deserts of Africa, the mountains of America, and the Arctic tundra. As soon as mammal scavengers find a carcass, they will feed on it. They aren't picky about the stage of decomposition the corpse is in and don't care if the insects have had their turn. Only a larger predator nearby can stop a mammal from eating a corpse.

Dominant scavengers such as wolves may eat the most, but furry death eaters work as a team to devour the carcass.

SQUIRRELS, SKUNKS, AND RACCOONS

Small mammals like squirrels, skunks, and raccoons are often the first noninsect death eaters to find the oozing carcass. Like all mammal scavengers, these three are opportunistic feeders—

they will eat what's available, even if that's a dead animal. Thinking of a squirrel as a death eater can be surprising. People generally believe that squirrels stick to certain foods, such as fruit, plants, and nuts. But squirrels are known for their curious behavior—they are willing to sample just about any kind of food—including carrion, the flesh of dead animals.

As with squirrels, skunks commonly eat nuts and berries. But skunks are also predators—they often hunt insects, snakes, and small rodents such as field mice and rabbits.

Raccoons don't just eat human garbage—they eat the dead too. This raccoon is feasting on a dead squirrel.

HUMAN DEATH EATERS

When a deer leaps out of the darkness and into a pair of headlights, a fast-moving vehicle can't always stop in time to save its life. But a growing number of new death eaters are stepping up to make use of the meat: humans.

In September 2016, Washington State joined Idaho and Montana and legalized the human consumption of fresh roadkill. "Why let the meat go to waste?" said Mick Cope of the Washington Department of Fish and Wildlife.

With a free permit, Washington citizens can salvage the deer (or other animals killed), bring it home, and process it as food—at their own risk. Permits do not guarantee the meat is fresh enough to be safe for human consumption, but when it is, it's a cheap way to keep freezers full.

While it is legal in many states (and many countries around the world), not all states are on board with human scavenging. But since up to three thousand deer and elk fall victim to vehicles in Washington State every year, eating their remains might be a practical way to clean up the waste.

A man collects a pheasant killed by a car in Kent, England.

Skunks can use their signature smelly spray for self-defense, but they aren't known to fight and kill animals larger than themselves. To avoid larger predators, they eat whatever they can get, including the meat of dead animals.

Of these three animals, raccoons are probably the best-known scavengers. They eat just about anything and everything, even garbage and carrion. Their diverse diet means raccoons can live—and thrive—in almost any location.

Together, along with other small mammals, squirrels, skunks, and raccoons play an important role in recycling the dead. And as they feed on small portions of meat, they create new, wet openings for mother blowflies to lay their eggs. This active decay creates more stink—stink larger mammals can't resist.

WOLVES, HYENAS, AND TASMANIAN DEVILS

Like almost all other mammal scavengers, wolves, hyenas, and Tasmanian devils are predators—they hunt and kill most of their food. But hunting is dangerous and exhausting work. If a meal of a dead animal is available, these carnivores will dig in.

Wolves, found in Africa, northern Asia, Europe, and North America, prefer colder climates. Hyenas, which are native to Africa and southern Asia, thrive in warmer areas. These two death eaters are very similar. Both wolves and hyenas are nocturnal—they sleep during the day and hunt at night. They are both pack animals too—they travel and hunt in groups.

When wolves and hyenas find the carcass of a dead animal, often one killed by a larger predator, they eat as much of the corpse as they can as quickly as possible. They'll also drag bits of the carcass back to their dens to eat later or to feed to their pups. Their keen eyesight, strong sense of smell, and instinct to travel in groups make wolves and hyenas formidable death eaters. Only a very large predator can scare them away from their meal.

Tasmanian devils eat every scrap of carrion, including hair and bones.

Unlike wolves and hyenas, Tasmanian devils—found on the Australian island of Tasmania—are solitary creatures. Though they are only the size of a small dog, Tasmanian devils are known for their violent temper and dirty fighting skills. They will hunt birds, fish, and insects, but they also eat carrion.

If more than one Tasmanian devil want the same dead animal, they will often fight with one another. When the dominant Tasmanian devil finally secures its meal, it will eat the whole carcass—flesh, hair, bones, and all. It won't waste the valuable food.

Although these medium-sized scavengers are strong, fast, and intelligent, they are no match for the largest death eaters.

AN ISLAND DEATH EATER

Mammals are usually the top predators on land, but just north of Australia on the Lesser Sunda Islands, a dragon is king. The Komodo dragon will eat virtually any meat, dead or alive, fresh or rancid, large or small.

Topping out at 10 feet (3 m) long and more than 300 pounds (136 kg), the Komodo dragon can hunt living prey with a sprint of 12 miles (19 km) an hour. But if the target of its hunt escapes with only a bite, the Komodo bides its time. Dragon saliva is so rich with deadly bacteria that the wounded animal rarely survives. Once it dies, the Komodo can feed at its own pace.

If live prey is scarce, this death eater isn't picky. Komodo dragons will simply smell a dead carcass, dig it up, and eat it—no species is off-limits, including humans. As an opportunistic feeder, the Komodo dragon will consume virtually anything that it can find.

The long, forked tongue of a Komodo dragon smells the air for carrion.

BEARS AND LIONS

Although big mammals such as bears and lions are skilled hunters, they are also opportunistic feeders—they know that scavenging is less dangerous than a hunt that could leave them injured. As their natural habitats shrink and food becomes scarce, already dead animals are an appealing alternative.

A mother grizzly bear that arrives at a dead carcass can easily drive away any smaller animals feeding on it. She'll claim the carcass as her own by hiding it under a mound of dirt or laying across it.

Stretched across the body, the grizzly bear might sound a warning, a pulsating growl that says, "This food is mine." The bear will fight off other animals that come for food, and when it's safe, she'll call for her babies to come eat too. She'll wander away only after she's eaten her fill.

A mother grizzly bear shares a dead salmon with her cub in Alaska.

Female lions handle most of the hunting. They aren't as fast or as large as their typical prey—antelope or zebras—so they hunt as a group. But lions aren't in a hurry. They spend between sixteen to twenty hours a day playing and napping. If they can overpower another carnivore, such as a cheetah, out of its meal or if they can eat a big animal that's already dead, lions will do it—this helps them conserve energy.

A PREHISTORIC DEATH EATER

For years, scientists debated an important question: Was the mighty *Tyrannosaurus rex* a hunter or a scavenger? Did it kill its food, or did it steal from other meat eaters? It seems the answer is both.

Paleontologist Robert DePalma made an important discovery that proves the T. *rex* was a predator. A T. *rex* tooth embedded in a hadrosaur's fossilized body proves the plant eater was alive during the fearsome hunter's attack. How can DePalma be sure? After the attack from the T. *rex*, the hadrosaur didn't die. It survived long enough to fully heal with the tooth still lodged in its tail, proving that the T. *rex* fed on the living.

But paleontologist Jack Horner says, "He has no arms, can't run fast, appears to have a large olfactory lobe, and he's big. Interestingly enough if you think about it, one of the best things to be if you are a scavenger is big so you can chase away anything else around the carcass." Even this king of the dinosaurs, a predator, scavenged sometimes!

Top: A T. rex tooth

Bottom: *An artist's rendering of T. rex*

Chapter 4

DEATH EATERS FROM THE SKY

Mammals are not the only animals drawn to decaying bodies. Many birds are death eaters too. Which creature feeds first often comes down to luck or the direction of the scent drifting in the wind. Whether furred or feathered, they contribute greatly to decomposition.

CROWS

Crows are master death eaters for two reasons: their intelligence and their strength as a flock.

According to the magazine *Audubon*, crows are similar to primates in their brainpower. Crows have large forebrains that allow them to reason and problem solve. For example, if a pair of crows find two wolves feasting on a carcass, the crows will stop before trying to take the carcass for themselves. Part of their pause comes from a practical standpoint: crow beaks aren't always sharp enough to break the skin of a tough hide, so they let the wolves make the first cuts into the carcass. The crows also know they cannot overcome the wolves on their own, so they rely on their second advantage: the size of their flock.

A pair of wolves can overpower two crows. But a wolf duo is no match for a massive flock of crows. With one clear signal, two crows can be joined by hundreds of allies to overwhelm their competition. If the rest of the flock is too far away to hear the cries, the crows dodge, dart, and steal food until the wolves have had their fill.

According to Richard Inger of the University of Exeter in England, crows may be the cleverest of scavenging birds. Inger and his research team put rat carcasses in twelve places on the university campus and then carefully observed what happened next. Seventeen kinds of death eaters fed on the rats, including buzzards, magpies, seagulls, foxes, and badgers. But a full 98 percent was eaten by crows.

"It's a bit grizzly," Inger said, "but crows . . . which are often perceived as

A group, or flock, of crows is called a murder.

pests . . . are performing a very valuable service. Without these scavengers, dead animals would be scattered around our environment, rotting and causing a hygiene hazard."

BALD EAGLES

Bald eagles are another feathered death eater. They use their strong talons to get most of their food from killing fish and small mammals such as rabbits and squirrels. But like many mammals, they are opportunistic predators. They'll steal prey from smaller animals, or they'll eat dead fish or mammals.

In late fall and winter in the Pacific Northwest region, migrating bald eagles—along with bears and other death eaters—descend in vast numbers to feed on hundreds of dead salmon. The schools of fish have returned to their birthplace to lay and fertilize eggs, and they die soon

A bald eagle eats a dead salmon in Alaska.

after reproducing. Pools of dead salmon would contaminate the river, creating massive health risks for life downstream. But bald eagles help clean up the bodies, and they use the nutrients from the salmon to fuel their own journey as they migrate south.

Much like the Tasmanian devil, bald eagles eat as much of the carrion as they can, including the bones, which their strong stomachs can digest.

TURKEY VULTURES

Turkey vultures are death eaters known for their keen sense of smell. "They track plumes of odor from decaying animals while gliding high in the air column," says Gary Graves, an ornithologist at the Smithsonian Institution. "Their sense of smell is so acute they can locate hidden food . . . as small as a dead rat under a pile of leaves."

Turkey vultures' powerful nostrils can smell death from 2 miles (3.2 km) away. The vultures prefer dead mammals, but they will eat dead fish or dead reptiles, if necessary. They can even consume contaminated meat other death eaters might avoid.

Turkey vultures (and vultures of all kinds) are different from other scavengers in a big way: they live almost exclusively on carrion, rarely killing their own food. Vultures are able to find enough food this way because they can eat even the most rotted kinds of flesh—flesh that other animals won't touch.

TOXIC AMMO

Hunting is a popular activity throughout the world. In many ways, hunting can be beneficial. But not all hunting habits are good.

Some hunters use toxic lead ammunition in their hunting rifles. Too much exposure to lead is deadly for many animals (including humans) because lead replaces other minerals that the body needs, such as zinc and iron.

Hunters don't collect all the animals shot with lead ammo. Some escape and then die. Those animals are scavenged by death eaters, which are then exposed to the lead.

According to hunter Steve Meyer, small mammals who eat the lead are immune to the danger. "Waterfowl hunters can tell you that unrecovered ducks are consumed largely by mink, weasels, or ermine," he says. "There seems to be no evidence that these animals were adversely affected in any significant way when we were still using lead shot."

Birds of prey, however, are not so lucky. Feathered scavengers who eat the lead along with the carrion meat are poisoned. For them, the exposure can be a death sentence.

How can turkey vultures survive eating all rotted flesh? According to the Cornell Lab of Ornithology, these death eaters have developed special immunities. Toxins like botulism, anthrax, cholera, and salmonella can kill other creatures. But the stomach acid in turkey vultures is extremely strong, so they can process the poison along with the food.

BEARDED VULTURES

As decomposition moves from advanced decay toward its last stage—dry remains—a new vulture steps in. When other scavengers have abandoned the bones, the bearded vulture finds more to harvest.

Bearded vultures are resourceful. If the bones they find are too large, they gather them in their talons, soar above their rocky nesting grounds, and drop the bones so that they crack against the stones. Then the bearded vultures spiral down to retrieve the broken shards and feed on a tasty treat.

Bone marrow is inside the core of the bone, and the bearded vultures gobble the protein from each fracture. But they don't eat only the bone marrow—they also eat tiny pieces of bone. Bearded vultures' stomach acid is so powerful that it can digest the bones. Bone marrow and bones provide the bearded vulture with 70 to 90 percent of the nutrients it needs to survive. The flesh from smaller dead animals make up the rest of its diet.

Top: *When a turkey vulture smells death from high in the air, it pinpoints the carcass by flying in circles above it before diving.*

Bottom: *A bearded vulture prepares to drop a bone on rocks below.*

Despite being creative scavengers, the population of bearded vultures is classified as near threatened. Only one hundred breeding pairs exist in the wild—mostly in the Pyrenees Mountains of France and Spain. The large birds were once feared and, therefore, hunted by humans. Ranchers also hunted bearded vultures because they thought the birds killed and fed on their livestock.

Conservationists are fighting to save the species through captive breeding, but poisons threaten their cause. Once the captives are rereleased in the wild, they are exposed to danger. Some sheep ranchers poison wolves for killing lambs, and bearded vultures feed on the poisonous remains of the wolves.

SEAGULLS

Seagulls may not be as majestic as bald eagles or as versatile as vultures. Many people see seagulls as only common picnic thieves on most beaches. But before garbage was common on beaches, gulls didn't feed on trash—they fed on death.

FEAR OF VULTURES

Even though most vultures do not kill their own food, many are slaughtered because of human fear. Farmers believe they'll feed on healthy livestock, and farmers kill the vultures to prevent it. But turkey vultures feed only on the kill of other predators—they clean up the dead—and killing them can cause new problems.

For example, when the Indian vulture population disappeared, wild dogs quickly stepped up to fill the role of death eater. Feral dogs are not vaccinated against diseases, and they are not spayed or neutered. As their pack sizes grow, so does human exposure to dangerous diseases such as rabies.

Feral dogs circle an animal carcass in India.

When creatures from the ocean die, their carcasses can wash ashore. Seagulls traditionally fed on those bodies. But as humans encroached on seagull habitats, their diet changed. They began to forage through human garbage.

Why the shift? Garbage is easy. Battling other scavengers for the dead body of a whale in the shallows can be very dangerous for a seagull. Gobbling trash is much simpler, especially since many humans feed seagulls.

SKY BURIAL

High in the mountains of Tibet and Mongolia, people who practice Vajrayana Buddhism observe a unique burial ritual. When a loved one dies, the corpse is taken to a place like the Larung Valley where spiritual leaders called monks pray over it and prepare it for sky burial.

Vajrayana Buddhists do not believe in preserving the body once the spirit has escaped it, so the monks feed the corpses to the vultures of the region.

Hundreds of the hungry death eaters gracefully descend, and within minutes, all the flesh is consumed. Family members are allowed to witness the sky burial, but tourists are not. As with most funeral practices, they are considered private ceremonies for the relatives of the deceased.

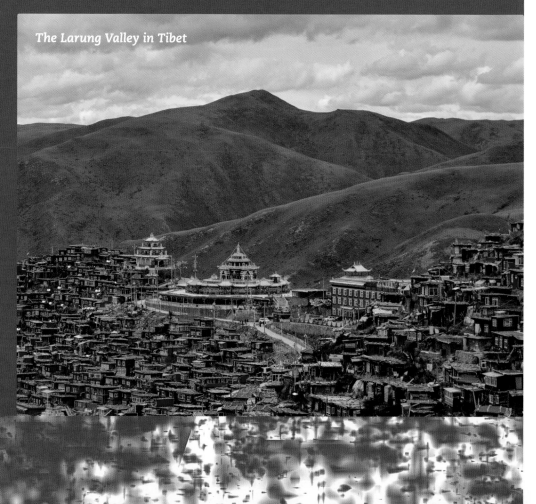
The Larung Valley in Tibet

While it might be nice to have seagulls helping to discard trash, the food is unhealthy for the gulls to eat and it leaves other dead animals to rot on the beach. According to microbiologist Elizabeth Wheeler Alm, "The only real way to keep them from scavenging human debris is to change how we discard things," she says. If we block their access to trash, seagulls will return to their death-eater ways.

Before seagulls had easy access to food in trash, they consumed dead marine life such as this cannonball jellyfish (upper right).

Chapter 5

DEATH EATERS IN THE SEA

Death eaters from the land and the sky are around to clean up the deceased carcasses on land, but what happens when life ends in the ocean? Since humans can't easily see into the depths, in many ways, it's a mystery. But scientists like Gail Anderson are searching for the answers.

CRUSTACEANS

A scientist at Simon Fraser University in Canada, Anderson and her colleague Lynne Bell lowered three different dead pigs into the Saanich Inlet near Vancouver Island in British Columbia. For three consecutive years—2006, 2007, and 2008—they submerged a new pig 330 feet (101 m) underwater using remote-controlled submarines. Video cameras and scientific sensors secured at the sites by VENUS—the Victoria Experimental Network under the Sea—made it possible for Anderson to monitor the carcasses in real time over the Internet.

The first two pigs were anchored firmly in the same spot in oxygen-rich water in 2006 and again in 2007. Almost immediately, three different kinds of scavengers—5-inch (13 cm) spot prawns, 8-inch (20 cm) Dungeness crabs, and 3-inch (7.6 cm) squat lobsters—were drawn to the first pig. Within just twenty-two days, the bones were bare and unanchored. The army of crustaceans was able to drag the remains clear of camera view. The crustaceans consumed the second pig in much the same way, but the third pig was another story.

Pig number 3 was put in the same place, but in 2008, the water had far less oxygen. With less air to process through their gills, the larger, more powerful crustaceans could not get to the carcass. For weeks the crustaceans ignored it. Small squat lobsters eventually tried to feast on the pig, but their tiny mouths were too weak to pierce the animal's skin.

A stringy coat of sulfur-rich bacteria soon covered the final pig, but the pig wasn't consumed until oxygen levels rose in the spring. Once it did, larger scavengers returned and picked the bones clean, ninety-two days after it was first offered.

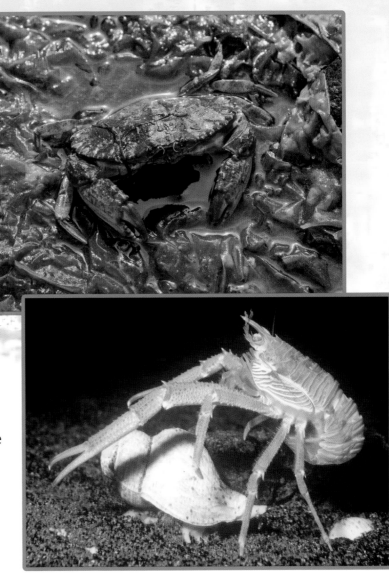

Dungeness crabs (top) and squat lobsters (bottom) are both death eaters of the sea.

Crustaceans such as lobsters and crabs are not picky eaters. They also aren't picky about where and when they eat. For example, lobsters are typically nocturnal, but sometimes they feed during the day if more food is available. Their flexibility and ability to eat many kinds of food (including plants, krill, and dead creatures) help them survive longer.

While crustaceans seem to be the first and most efficient death eaters in the ocean, they are far from alone. In deeper water, the shark may be the ultimate king.

GREENLAND SHARK

"Sharks, like any predators, are opportunistic feeders," says George Burgess, director of the Florida Program for Shark Research at the Florida Museum of Natural History in Gainesville. "They'll take advantage of a resource that's given to them," even if that resource is dead.

The shark most likely to be a death eater—the Greenland shark—is something of a mystery itself. At 24 feet (7.3 m) long, it is one of the largest fish in the sea, but it is hard to find. It isn't a fast swimmer—its cruising speed is less than 1 mile (1.6 km) per hour. But it can hide from curious humans in plain sight, thanks to its deep-sea habitat.

Greenland sharks thrive in deep, frigid waters that few human divers are likely to explore. But when scientists seek them out, they find many of them. And they usually find them partially blind, thanks to a tiny crustacean that feeds on the sharks' eyes. How does a big, slow, visually impaired shark find enough to eat? It feeds on the dead.

Anything that falls into Arctic waters can be a tasty morsel for the scavenger. Two men in Newfoundland, Canada, once rescued a beached Greenland shark choking on a moose.

A Greenland shark swims under a layer of ice. Attached to its eye is a crustacean known as Ommatokoita elongata. This parasite, which feeds on the shark's eye, is less than

SLEEPING WITH THE FISHES

Did you know some people choose to be buried at sea?

Burial at sea is an Earth-friendly way to dispose of a dead body. Embalming chemicals—like formaldehyde and glutaraldehyde—and protective coffins are typically used when burying a body in a US cemetery. Both the chemicals and the coffin are meant to delay decomposition, protecting the families of the dead from seeing their loved one's body decay. But these materials can be very expensive.

Neither chemicals nor coffins are required for burial at sea in the United States, however. A simple biodegradable canvas shroud and a cannonball (to weigh down the body) usually replace the costly materials needed for burials on land.

What happens to the body in the sea? Once the canvas shroud unravels, the body feeds the whole range of aquatic death eaters. But people who choose this option are OK with being fish food. "Typically, they have a love for the ocean," says Brad White, a ship captain who buries bodies in the Atlantic Ocean. "They want to become part of the Earth again."

Americans have been slow to warm up to the idea of being buried at sea. But families in other parts of the world are encouraged to use this option—in fact, the Chinese government helps families pay for burial at sea.

US sailors conduct a burial at sea aboard the USS McClusky.

Derrick Chaulk was driving along the Atlantic coast when he spotted what he thought was a beached whale. When he ran to its aid, he realized it was a Greenland shark in distress. A large piece of moose was lodged in its throat.

Chaulk and Jeremy Ball pulled the moose from the shark's giant jaws and then carefully rolled the mammoth creature back into the water. Greenland shark expert Jeffrey Gallant commends the heroic Canadians but offers an important suggestion: next time, leave the moose in the shark's mouth. "That way," he told CBC News, "you reduce the risk of getting bit accidentally."

Perhaps but Chaulk has no regrets. "It was a good feeling to see that shark swim out," he said, "knowing that we saved his life." Though scientists can't say for certain, the belief has been that most sharks prefer to kill their food rather than eat the bodies of dead animals. But scientists have recently learned that great white sharks will eat the blubber (or fat) from a whale carcass. Tiger sharks also have been discovered eating dead green turtles.

BONE-EATING WORMS

Do tiny death eaters glide through the sea as they do on solid ground? Maggots don't exist underwater, but another worm steps up to tackle whalebones when the flesh has been cleared. Bone-eating worms called *Osedax* scour the deep seafloor to feed on sunken treasure. They look like blowfly maggots, but unlike maggots, *Osedax* feed on a carcass at the end of decomposition, not at the beginning.

About 10,000 feet (3,048 m) below the ocean's surface, the female *Osedax* eats fat and protein trapped within a whalebone. Acids in her skin dissolve the whalebones, freeing up the nutrients. But the worms can't digest those nutrients on their own.

Bacteria trapped in the *Osedax* roots—like legs— digest the food as the worms drill into the bone. Once the bacteria digestion is complete, the bacteria pass the nutrients to the *Osedax*. Fluttering red fringe on the back end of the *Osedax* gathers oxygen from the water, so the bacteria can feed and breathe at the same time.

After other death eaters eat the flesh of dead marine animals, Osedax devour the bones.

If the plumes of fringe are disturbed, the bacteria retreat into the worm's body for safety.

Where are the male *Osedax* while the females scavenge for food? More than a hundred microscopic males live inside the female worm's body, ready to fertilize her eggs when it's time to continue the species.

Scientists from the Monterey Bay Aquarium Research Institute first discovered these bone-eating ocean worms in 2002. The worms' preferred diet is debatable. Some scientists believe *Osedax* feed only on whalebones. Others say they feed on whatever they can find, including fish bones and cow bones dumped as garbage from ships. Scientists are hoping to learn more through further study.

TEENY-TINY DEATH EATERS

After the animal scavengers have eaten their fill, a new squad of death eaters, called decomposers, take over. Mainly bacteria and fungi, decomposers are small, but they have a big job to do. Like all animals, they cannot make their own food, so decomposers survive by feeding on dead plants and animals as well as animal feces. Bacteria and fungi break down the dead through biochemical reactions, and these reactions release nutrients such as carbon and nitrogen back into the ecosystem. Surrounding soil and plants absorb the nutrients. Decomposers play a big role in keeping ecosystems healthy as they clean up the dead and free up nutrients that help nourish the living.

Fungi break down and digest the body of a moth.

DEATH AFTER LIFE

I am sixty years old—closer to my death than to my birth. But I remember being a kid as if it were yesterday.

When I was about eight years old, I found a dead kitten in my tree house. I cried, looking at its tiny, lifeless body. I took it to my father, and he helped me bury it as I wept.

"What will happen to it?" I asked him.

My father explained the body would decompose and disappear. That day his explanation was enough for me. But for days after, I grieved over that kitten's death and tried to imagine what was unfolding underground. I wanted to dig it up to see, but I couldn't bear what that might reveal. I was trapped between curiosity and fear.

I finally confessed, and my father gathered me up in his strong arms to reassure me. "Never be ashamed of wondering," he said. Then he told me about how death eaters would break down and recycle the kitten's body.

I was still sad about that kitten. But that his little life had meaning and that he was feeding so many creatures made his death feel less wasteful and less cruel.

As you can probably tell, I'm still fascinated by the animals that live by eating the dead. I hope this book will help you see the beauty of life and death in a whole new way. And like me, I hope that learning about decomposition will fill you with wonder.

SOURCE NOTES

13   Jennifer L. Pechal, telephone interview with the author, April 4, 2017.

14   Marla Vacek Broadfoot, "Ask a Scientist: What Is a Coffin Fly?," *News & Observer* (Raleigh, NC), last modified June 15, 2015, http://www.newsobserver.com/news/technology/article23720968.html.

17   Tom Banse, "Washington State Legalizes Roadkill Salvage, Oregon Still Firmly Forbids," *Northwest News Network*, September 2, 2016, http://nwnewsnetwork.org/post/washington-state-legalizes-roadkill-salvage-oregon-still-firmly-forbids.

21   John R. Horner, "Steak Knives, Beady Eyes, and Tiny Little Arms (a Portrait of T. *rex* as a Scavenger)," *The Paleontological Society Special Publication* 7 (1994): 157–164.

23–24   Richard Inger, Esra Per, Daniel T. C. Cox, and Kevin J. Gaston, "Key Role in Ecosystem Functioning of Scavengers Reliant on a Single Common Species," *Scientific Reports* 6 (July 2016), https://phys.org/news/2016-07-scavenger-crows.html.

25   John Barret, "Study Shows Turkey Vulture Is Doubly Blessed with Acute Vision and Sense of Smell," *Smithsonian Insider*, November 14, 2013, http://insider.si.edu/2013/11/study-shows-turkey-vulture-doubly-blessed-with-acute-vision-and-sense-of-smell/.

25   Steve Meyer, "A Hunter Does Some Soul Searching on the Issue of Toxic Ammo," *Anchorage Daily News*, March 21, 2017, https://www.adn.com/outdoors-adventure/2017/03/21/hunters-dilemma-soul-searching-on-the-non-toxic-ammo-issue/.

29   Jennifer S. Holland, "Gulls Be Gone: 10 Ways to Get Rid of Pesky Birds," *National Geographic*, June 10, 2014, http://news.nationalgeographic.com/news/2014/06/140610-birds-seagulls-deterrent-pollution-disease-sheepdog-raptor-beach/.

32   Brendan Borrell, "How Long Do Dead Bodies Remain Intact in the Ocean?," *Scientific American*, June 10, 2009, https://blogs.scientificamerican.com/news-blog/how-long-do-dead-bodies-remain-inta-2009-06-10/.

33   Dave Gilson, "What Happens When You're Buried at Sea," *Mother Jones*, May 9, 2011, http://www.motherjones.com/environment/2011/05/bin-laden-burial-at-sea.

34   Daniel D. Snyder, "Canadians Rescue Shark Choking on Moose," *Outside*, November 22, 2013, https://www.outsideonline.com/1800101/canadians-rescue-shark-choking-moose.

34   Ibid.

GLOSSARY

ashen: gray in color

autolysis: self-digestion; the breaking down of tissue by enzymes within that tissue

bacteria: one-celled organisms involved in chemical transformation of organic tissue or the spread of infectious diseases

biochemical reaction: a transformation of change in living things

biodegradable: capable of being broken down by natural processes

cadaver: a dead human body used for medical or scientific study

carcass: a dead body of an animal or human

carrion: flesh of dead animals generally unfit for human consumption

corpse: a dead body of an animal or human

crustacean: an animal that has a hard shell and lives in water, such as a crab or lobster

ecosystem: a community of living things interacting with their environment

endangered: used to describe a plant or animal that is rare and could die out

enzyme: a chemical substance in plants and animals that helps assist natural processes

ester: a strong-smelling organic compound formed when acid and other elements combine to release liquids

fungi: living things such as molds or mushrooms that look like plants but live on dead or decaying things

hadrosaur: a duck-billed, plant-eating dinosaur

hide: the skin of an animal

nutrient: a substance that is good for a living thing

olfactory lobe: a section of the brain that senses smells

opportunistic feeder: an animal that eats whatever food is available

predator: an animal that lives by killing and eating other animals

shroud: a cloth that wraps a dead body

spiracle: a breathing hole

tsunami: a large sea wave caused by an earthquake or volcanic eruption

vasodilation: dilation or widening of blood vessels

SELECTED BIBLIOGRAPHY

Anderson, Gail S. "Decomposition and Invertebrate Colonization of Cadavers in Coastal Marine Environments." In *Current Concepts in Forensic Entomology*, edited by Jens Amendt, Carlo P. Capobasso, and Martin Grassberger, 223–272. New York: Springer, 2010.

Anderson, Gail S., and Lynne S. Bell. "Deep Coastal Marine Taphonomy: Investigation into Carcass Decomposition in the Saanich Inlet, British Columbia Using a Baited Camera." *PLoS ONE* 9, no. 10 (October 2014). https://doi.org/10.1371/journal.pone.0110710.

Bass, William M., and Jon Jefferson. *Death's Acre: Inside the Legendary Forensic Lab the Body Farm Where the Dead Do Tell Tales.* New York: Putnam, 2003.

Gray, Richard. "The Fruity Stench of Human Death: Distinct 'Chemical Cocktail' Released by Dead Bodies Smells Like Berries and Apples." *Daily Mail* (London), September 23, 2015. http://www.dailymail.co.uk /sciencetech/article-3246192/The-fruity-stench-human-death-Distinct-chemical-cocktail-released-dead-bodies -smells-like-berries-apples.html.

Koehler, Steven A., and Cyril H. Wecht. *Postmortem: Establishing the Cause of Death.* Buffalo: Firefly Books, 2006.

Pechal, Jennifer L., M. Eric Benbow, Jeffery K. Tomberlin, Tawni L. Crippen, Aaron M. Tarone, Baneshwar Singh, and Paul A. Lenhart. "Field Documentation of Unusual Post-Mortem Arthropod Activity on Human Remains." *Journal of Medical Entomology*, January 2015. https://academic.oup.com/jme/article-abstract/doi/10.1093/jme /tju012/873303/Field-Documentation-of-Unusual-Post-Mortem?redirectedFrom=fulltext.

FURTHER READING

Books

Johnson, Rebecca L. *Zombie Makers: True Stories of Nature's Undead.* Minneapolis: Millbrook Press, 2013.

Murray, Elizabeth A. *Death: Corpses, Cadavers, and Other Grave Matters.* Minneapolis: Twenty-First Century Books, 2010.

Pressberg, Dava. *Producers, Consumers, and Decomposers.* New York: PowerKids, 2017.

Website and Videos

American Burying Beetle Fact Sheet
https://www.fws.gov/midwest/endangered/insects/ambb/abb_fact.html
Learn more about the endangered burying beetles and their impact as death eaters.

BBC Nature Wildlife
http://www.bbc.co.uk/nature/adaptations/Scavenger#p00ztzkf
This collection of videos examines the lives of scavengers and decomposers from all kinds of environments.

Valley of the Wolves
https://www.youtube.com/watch?v=nU2a3Z-ueMY
In this video, discover how wolves scavenge for their food and compete with other kinds of animals.

INDEX

PHOTO ACKNOWLEDGMENTS

Image credits: Kovalchuk Oleksandr/Shutterstock.com, pp. 1, 3, 38; Kletr/Shutterstock.com, pp. 2, 40; Haavard Kjoentvedt/Norwegian Nature Inspectorate/NTB scanpix/Newscom, p. 5; Biophoto Associates/Science Source, p. 7 (top); Science Photo Library - STEVE GSCHMEISSNER/Brand X Pictures/Getty Images, p. 7 (bottom); TJC/Moment Open/Getty Images, p. 8; AFP/Getty Images, p. 9; JJ Harrison/Wikimedia Commons (CC BY-SA 3.0), p. 11 (top); Stephen Dalton/Minden Pictures/Getty Images, p. 11 (middle); Laura Westlund/Independent Picture Service, p. 11 (bottom); KAREN BLEIER/AFP/Getty Images, p. 12; Kenneth H Thomas/Science Source/Getty Images, p. 13 (top); © Robert Pickett/Visuals Unlimited, Inc., p. 13 (bottom); © Joel Sartore/National Geographic Stock, p. 14 (bottom); Frank Hecker/Alamy Stock Photo, p. 14 (top); © Jason Edwards/National Geographic Stock, p. 15; Ivan Kuzmin/Alamy Stock Photo, p. 17 (top); Stuart Freedman/Getty Images, p. 17 (bottom); Rafael Ben-Ari/Chameleons Eye/Getty Images, p. 18; Cyril Ruoso/ Minden Pictures/Getty Images, p. 19; Biosphoto/Patrick Kientz/Getty Images, p. 20; Crazytang/iStock/Getty Images Plus/Getty Images, p. 21 (top); ROGER HARRIS/SPL/Getty Images, p. 21 (bottom); W. Wisniewsk/Corbis Documentary/Getty Images, p. 23; MIKHAIL MORDASOV/AFP/Getty Images, p. 23 (inset); Peter Mather/Minden Pictures/Getty Images, p. 24; Marsan/Shutterstock.com, p. 25; Larry Ditto/DanitaDelimont.com/Getty Images, p. 26 (top); AOosthuizen/iStock /Getty Images Plus/Getty Images, p. 26 (bottom); NurPhoto/Getty Images, p. 27; Xue Bin/VCG/Getty Images, p. 28; kcpetersen/iStock/Getty Images Plus/Getty Images, p. 29; John Dreyer/Moment Open/Getty Images, p. 29 (inset); Danita Delimont/Gallo Images/Getty Images, p. 31 (top); © Ken Lucas/Visuals Unlimited, Inc., p. 31 (bottom); Franco Banfi/WaterFrame/Getty Images, p. 32; Stocktrek Images, Inc./Alamy Stock Photo, p. 33; The Natural History Museum/Alamy Stock Photo, p. 34; Ian Redding/Getty Images, p. 35; dabjola/Shutterstock.com, p. 36; Tobyphotos/Shutterstock.com, p. 37.

Cover: Ger Bosma/Moment Open/Getty Images (vulture); dabjola/Shutterstock.com (larva); Kovalchuk Oleksandr/Shutterstock.com (larvae).